Helping at Home

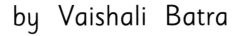

by Vaishali Batra

OXFORD
UNIVERSITY PRESS
AUSTRALIA & NEW ZEALAND

Jobs at Home

Do you do jobs at home?
You might pick up toys or help in
the garden.

At times, you might do jobs to get fun things.

What sort of jobs do you do?

Joe's Jobs

Joe asked for a new pet.
Dad said that Joe had to do a few jobs first.

He picked up toys and made his bed. He helped his dad make a cake. The next day, Dad gave Joe a fish!

Audrey's Jobs

Audrey asked her gran for a new game.
Gran said she needed to help out first.

Audrey used the hose to spray the car.
She gave the wheels a wipe too.
Gran gave her a cool new game!

Steph's Jobs

Steph's mum broke her leg.
She asked Steph to help.

Steph did jobs in the garden.
She used the **rake** and
then came the broom.
Mum said she was a big help.

Harvey's Jobs

Harvey hoped to help an **orphan** elephant.

He did a few jobs to get some coins.

Help this elephant.

He threw the dog a bone.
He gave its **coat** a brush.
He got some coins and
helped the elephant!

Paula's Jobs

Paula asked for a notebook
with a **lock** and key.
Pop asked her to do a few jobs.

First, she had to **complete** her reading. Next, she made notes on the computer. Then she handed it in to Mr Whitson. Paula got a red and white striped notebook from Pop!

Help at Home

What sort of jobs do you do?

Look It Up

coat: the fur on a pet

complete: finish

lock: it keeps a thing shut

orphan: a person without a mum or dad

rake: a tool used in the garden

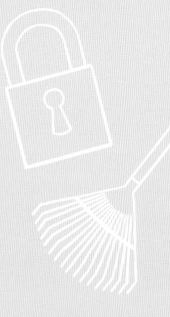

Index

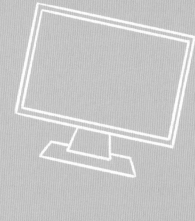